Contents

KU-078-722

Managing Your People

Fast Track to Business Excellence

Other books in the series:

Mastering Change

Outstanding Leadership

Exceptional Entrepreneurship

Managing Your People

Real-Life Lessons from Top Business Leaders

Adapted from the Fifty Lessons
management collection

Published by BBC Books,
BBC Worldwide Limited,
Woodlands, 80 Wood Lane,
London W12 0TT

First published 2005
Copyright © Fifty Lessons, 2005

The moral right of the author has been asserted.

ISBN: 0563 51937 1

Commissioning Editor
Emma Shackleton
Editors for Fifty Lessons
Adam Sodowick and **Jenny Watts**
Editor
Sarah Sutton
Designer
Andrew Barron @ Thextension
Typesetter
Kevin O'Connor
Production Controller
Man Fai Lau

Set in Clarendon Light and Scala sans
Printed and bound in Great Britain by
Goodman Baylis

Acknowledgements

We would like to thank all of the executives who have contributed their hard-won lessons to the Fifty Lessons business library.

We believe that recording the first-hand learning experiences of today's business leaders will prove to be of immeasurable value to the business leaders of the future.

We'd also like to thank all those who have believed in, and contributed their time to, this growing and exciting initiative. Your support has been invaluable.

From the team at Fifty Lessons

About Fifty Lessons

Wherever you are on the career ladder, you are walking in the footsteps of others. Whatever business dilemma you are facing, some of the finest brains in business have faced it before.

Fifty Lessons was born out of a desire to learn from the experience of today's greatest business minds. We felt that decades of hard-won business experience were being written off to the vagaries of memory and resolved to capture, store and pass on this wisdom to the next generation.

Using the power of storytelling, we have captured on film the most valuable and defining experiences of some of the biggest names in international business, and built them into a digital library containing over 400 lessons.

The *Fast Track to Business Excellence* series features specially chosen lessons from this library, offering inspiration, practical help and guidance across a diverse range of management challenges. In business, as in life, learning from the knowledge of others is invaluable. We believe that there is no substitute for experience.

Adam Sodowick
Co-founder

For access to filmed interviews from the entire Fifty Lessons management collection, please visit: www.fiftylessons.com

Introduction to Managing Your People

People are an organization's most valuable asset, and managing, motivating and retaining them sets a broad range of challenges for any manager to master. Effective managers improve communication, set clear strategic goals, empower their teams, and are tough when necessary.

Managing Your People gives you access to the real-life business experience of thirteen of today's outstanding business leaders in a pocket-sized format. Their personal stories, and how they learnt from their experiences, provide you with winning strategies and a fast track to understanding the best approaches to managing your people.

This book gives a unique insight into the role of the manager, the need for personal enthusiasm and how valuing your people will increase personal loyalty and improve performance. It exposes the hard realities of effective people management, especially in times of change, and the particular issues relating to managing high-maintenance individuals and letting people go. The book ends on the importance of planning your succession to safeguard the future stability of the business.

Whatever your level of management experience, these personal stories will provide you with invaluable knowledge, insight and understanding of how best to manage your people.

Focus on an individual's assets and how they can be of benefit to the company, rather than on their shortcomings. Developing people is an investment not to be written off lightly.

1 **The Head Gardener**
Lord Sharman

Chairman, *Aegis Group*; former Chairman, *KPMG International*

My Career

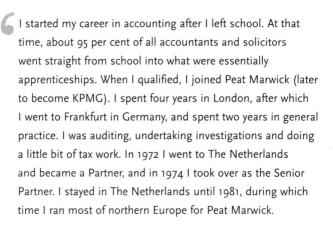

I started my career in accounting after I left school. At that time, about 95 per cent of all accountants and solicitors went straight from school into what were essentially apprenticeships. When I qualified, I joined Peat Marwick (later to become KPMG). I spent four years in London, after which I went to Frankfurt in Germany, and spent two years in general practice. I was auditing, undertaking investigations and doing a little bit of tax work. In 1972 I went to The Netherlands and became a Partner, and in 1974 I took over as the Senior Partner. I stayed in The Netherlands until 1981, during which time I ran most of northern Europe for Peat Marwick.

In 1981, back in London, I had various spells in setting up the government practice, the public sector practice, marketing – when the rules on accounting were relaxed – and then became head of the consulting practice both in the UK and worldwide. I followed that appointment by taking over as the Senior Partner of KPMG in London and the south, which was by far the biggest piece of KPMG in the UK. I became Chairman of KPMG in the UK, and then Chairman of KPMG International. I retired in September 1999.

From that point on I embarked on what headhunters call a portfolio career. I also went to the House of Lords. I undertook some government work, including a big investigation into the audit and accountability for the public sector in the twenty-first century. I sit currently as Chairman of Aegis, which is a big independent media group and am Deputy

Non-executive Chairman of Group 4 Securicor, the global network of security operations. I'm on the Boards of Aviva, the insurance company, Reed Elsevier, the publishers, and the BG Group, which is a gas exploration company. I'm on the supervisory board of ABN AMRO, the bank, and I get a lot of satisfaction from being Chairman of the advisory board of Good Corporation, which is a kitemark of corporate social responsibility for small and medium-sized companies.

Lord Sharman

Chairman, *Aegis Group*; former Chairman, *KPMG International*

The role of a manager is like that of a head gardener… to decide what qualities you will need in the plants you are choosing to grow.

As a manager it is important to focus on the strengths of an individual and concentrate on what they are good at, rather than what they're not so good at. The reason is that you can't build on a weakness. A weakness can be taken into account, but the way to get superior performance out of a group of people is to figure out what each of them is good at, and then ensure that each person is working in a role that uses that skill to the maximum advantage.

I'm very fond of gardening and gardening examples. In many ways the role of the manager is like that of a head gardener. To some degree developing people in an organization is impossible – because you can't develop people: they develop themselves. Your role is to figure out what the various microclimates are around the office and then to decide what qualities you will need in the plants you are choosing to grow in those microclimates. Then you select the plants – in the form of your people – based on their strengths, and place them in those jobs. I've seen notes made following appraisal interviews that show that two-thirds of the interview was spent talking about what the guy's not good at. Now that can only be counter-productive. I can't imagine anybody coming out of an interview like that feeling anything other than very depressed.

How much more constructive it is to spend time talking about what the person is good at, and how he's going to develop his strengths. Of course discuss whether you can do something to address the weaknesses, but to my way of thinking two-thirds of the appraisal interview should be about what the person is good at, and how those great assets can be used within the organization.

Two-thirds of the appraisal interview should be about what the person is good at, and how those great assets can be used within the organization.

If you look at good coaches in the sports field – and I've always been fascinated by how good coaches operate – you'll notice that they don't actually coach technique very often. The really effective coaches are the ones who coach the mind and work on improving personal attitude. You will always have people who find it much easier to be critical than to be encouraging. The tone coming from the top of the management ladder has got to be right. If the person at the top starts to criticize colleagues and focuses mainly on what they're bad at, rather than being encouraging, then that attitude is going to spread down through the organization very quickly.

When I was at KPMG I insisted that one of the senior guys should meet every new person joining the organization. It didn't matter whether they were a typist, telephonist, a graduate recruit or somebody being brought in as a senior manager: the induction programmes were always attended by people at the top level of the organization. I used to do half a dozen a year myself.

Effective coaches are the ones who coach the mind and work on improving personal attitude.

In some organizations, mentoring is well established and extremely important. It may spawn the notion that your career is unlikely to progress unless you work for a particular individual, and that you have to work for them to get on. I don't think that environment is very desirable, but I do think that having access to someone in the organization who takes an interest in you is a positive thing. A mentor can help you over the bad times, as well encouraging you through the good. This is very important, particularly to young individuals, and is also vital in planning to retain people.

In people-based industries, every time you lose somebody you're losing an investment. People don't like me saying this, but it's like writing off a piece of new plant. If you had to write off a production facility because it was no longer useful to you, people would get quite exercised about the impact on the accounts. If you lose ten young men or women whom you've spent the last five years developing, you are losing just as big an investment; it just doesn't show up on the balance sheet.

1966	**Peat Marwick Mitchell (later KPMG)** *Manager* Worked in a number of overseas offices before being appointed a Partner.
1981	*Partner* – London branch
1987–1990	Responsible for the group's national marketing.
1990–1991	Responsible for operations in London and the southeast.
1991–1994	**KPMG Management Consulting worldwide** *Chairman* One of the world's 'big four' companies in accounting.
1994	**KPMG (UK)** *Senior Partner* Served as a member of the International Executive Committee and on the European Board.
1997–1999	**KPMG International** *Chairman*
1999	**Aegis Group** Appointed to the Board of this independent media group.
1999	Awarded a life peerage.
2000–present	*Chairman*
2003–2004	**Securicor** *Chairman* Securicor was a leading security services company.
2004–present	**Group 4 Securicor** *Deputy Non-executive Chairman* Group 4 Securicor is a leading international security services company created after Group 4 Falck's security business merged with Securicor.

Identifying leaders
is about picking the
right strategic thinker,
developing that person,
then giving them
the coaching and
framework in which
to be successful.

2a **Identifying and Developing Leaders**
Neil Holloway

Corporate Vice President, Sales, Marketing and Services, *Microsoft EMEA*

My Career

I went to Bath University where I studied mathematics for four years; then I spent a year studying operational research at Cambridge. My supervisor was a professor who had just started his own computer company, so I ended up working for him while I was finishing my studies. I stayed with his company for about two or three years.

I then moved to a larger software company, where I had a technical sales role for a couple of years before being headhunted by two or three people from the USA to set up Ferguson Software Space. I ran that company for about eighteen months. Then, about fourteen years ago, I had to make a decision to join either a company called Sun or another company called Microsoft. I think the gods were smiling on me that day: I joined Microsoft.

Once inside Microsoft I had a variety of different roles: sales and marketing; looking after the enterprise customers; taking care of the small to medium-sized customers; managing marketing groups. I became Deputy Managing Director after about four or five years, then ran the UK subsidiary for about six years. I started my present job about a year ago and my current title is Corporate Vice President for Sales, Marketing and Services EMEA (Europe, Middle East and Africa).

Neil Holloway

Corporate Vice President: Sales, Marketing and Services, *Microsoft EMEA*

The better leaders are at selecting the right people, developing those people, and giving them the right framework within which to be successful, the more successful they will be.

What makes a great leader? I think that great leaders tend to be strong in three core areas – not just one or two, but three.

One core strength surrounds the area of strategic thinking and leadership. Some people may be very good at thinking and less skilled at leadership; some may be very good only at strategic leadership. In order to select the right people for management and leadership positions it is important when recruiting to articulate clearly what your business strategy is, where you want to head as a company, what directions you can set for your people, and what relationships you want to have with business partners.

The second core strength relates to people. The better leaders are at selecting the right people, developing those people, and giving them the right framework within which to be successful, the more successful they will be.

The third core strength relates to a willingness to 'roll the sleeves up'. A study of leaders who have been very successful

shows that the difference between success and failure
is related not just to having a good idea, but also to the
execution of the idea.

Great leaders are able to achieve a balance between strategic
thought and hands-on leadership. From a people perspective,
they have a skill for hiring, developing and motivating the
right individuals. They also have the ability to ensure that
ideas are executed in a quick, crisp way, while providing an
environment that enables people to learn what didn't work,
as well as what did.

How is it best to develop leaders in a company? First,
identify the attributes of a great leader; second, identify that
potential in the people the company hires; third, coach them.
After that, it's important to make sure that people are put
into a situation where they can learn and be coached in an
ongoing fashion.

Looking back over the years, I see many examples within our
company where somebody who was good in one particular
area, such as a traditional channel, has been put into a
completely new business area, like the consumer business

It's important to make sure that
people are put into a situation where
they can learn and be coached in an
ongoing fashion.

In order to deliver excellence, as well as to be a good leader, it is necessary to make sure that you, as leader, do not do everything yourself, or tell people how to do everything.

or our gaming console. In their new role we've coached them through their thinking, through the way they might approach their new post, how they could approach strategic development, and have provided guidance on the hiring process and how to select people. Through all this we do not tell them what to do; we coach them.

Whether focusing on new starters or people who've been with the company for ten years, we listen to what they're trying to achieve and also make sure that they understand what the big picture is, but without providing too much detail. In order to deliver excellence, as well as to be a good leader, it is necessary to make sure that you, as leader, do not do everything yourself, or tell people how to do everything.

Leadership is about identifying talent and then developing that talent. At Microsoft, the way we develop talent is not through any outside business school, but by stretching people, by putting them into very challenging roles, and also by ensuring that there is a coach to help them grow through the learning process.

To empower your people
you must create a
common vision of what
you want to achieve
and then show them
how they can make that
happen. Once people
understand what their
contribution is, they will
feel very empowered.

Empower Your People to Deliver

It's the individuals and the teams that are going to make it work, not the business leaders.

Towards the end of the dot-com era there was a lot of talk about e-government. Governments dreamt of being able to deliver great services to their citizens, and everybody around the world was looking for the pilot projects that would highlight which government would take the lead and make that first step towards finding an e-solution.

At that time the UK government was looking to deliver what it called the Government Gateway, which was to be the cornerstone of its strategy to start building e-services for citizens. Delivery of the concept was put out to tender, and was to include the delivery of the service, building the system and running the portal. The company that was short-listed got two-thirds of the way down the line towards delivery when, with about four or five months to go, they decided that they couldn't deliver what they'd been asked to do. This was our moment to seize the situation and say: 'We have enough faith in our technology, enough faith in our people and our partners, to step up to the plate and know that we can deliver something on time that will more than meet your expectations.'

When you win a big deal, such as the Government Gateway, how do you make it work? The answer is to approach it

Empowering people is about creating an environment that enables them to take responsibility for their actions and be accountable.

as you would any other project and any other business relationship. All you can do is create a common vision with regard to what you're trying to achieve, and then make sure that you create an environment in house that encourages your people to buy into the process, because it's the individuals and the teams who are going to make it work, not the business leaders. Once the leaders have created the working environment, success becomes about making sure that the vision is understood, that each person understands what their contribution is and that, when a successful outcome is achieved, they celebrate their success.

With so much at stake, how is it possible to create a working environment that allows people to make mistakes and learn from them, yet still feel they can be part of the overall end-game? Part of that just comes down to the leader's judgement with regard to understanding the working framework that is being created: ensuring that people understand what is at stake, what their personal boundaries are, what kinds of risks they can take and when they need to ask for external input, perhaps even for the ultimate decision. Empowering people is about creating an environment that enables them to take responsibility for their actions and be accountable. It is important when a mistake is made for the coach to go back to the individual concerned and make sure the person understands what has happened, that they understand the consequences of their action, and enable them to continue, rather than playing the blame game or telling them that their actions have destroyed the whole process.

Developing effective leaders comes down to adopting an effective style of coaching, as opposed to a style of leading, in order to build trust and let things happen. You have to let things happen. If you're going to hire bright people and enable them to do some great work, you've got to give them some rope – not to hang themselves with, but rope to go wandering.

I think what I managed to do when working on the Government Gateway was to create an environment where people felt empowered. It was not micro-management, although people did have to report back every couple of weeks with regard to what was going on. I learned to take the risk of committing to the client and then to ensure we created the right environment to enable the team, which was a very smart bunch of people, to deliver. It's important to ensure that people feel comfortable with the style of leadership they're getting because the trust element is very important. ""

Executive Timeline Neil Holloway

Early years	Degree in mathematics, Bath University
	Masters degree, Cambridge University
Early career	**Ashton Tate**
	Business Development Manager
	Ashton Tate was the original developer and vendor of the dBASE relational database and application development tool. In the early 1990s it was taken over by Borland International Inc.
	Migent UK
	Managing Director
	A company operating in the consumer and client server software markets.
	Ferguson Software Space
	Chief Executive
1990	**Microsoft Corporation**
	The world's largest manufacturer of computer software.
	Since joining the company, has held a number of strategic roles within Microsoft EMEA (Europe, Middle East and Africa) and the UK subsidiary.
	Manager – Enterprise Customer Unit
	Director – Organization Customer Unit
	Deputy Managing Director – Microsoft UK
1998	*Managing Director* – Microsoft UK
2000	*Vice President* – Microsoft EMEA
2003–present	*Vice President* – Sales, Marketing and Services: EMEA

> A business is built by people, not bricks and mortar. Communicating with passion inspires employees and instils a real sense of ownership in the business.

3 **Passion**

Perween Warsi

Founder and Chief Executive Officer, *S&A Foods*

My Career

I started S&A Foods in 1986. I was a housewife at the time, with two young children aged eight and nine and plenty of time on my hands. It was a period when so-called Indian foods were coming into the market. I felt very disappointed that they were not authentic and said to myself: 'Somebody has to take responsibility for putting this situation right, and it might as well be me.' I began by making finger foods, such as samosas and kebabs, and taking them to a local take-away. I was very pleased when the food sold well from day one.

My aim from the outset was to make my products available throughout the nation so that everyone would be able to buy and enjoy them. The key to achieving this was to find a way into the supermarket chains because they have stores nationwide. I started knocking on their doors and it all evolved from there. It all happened very, very quickly: I was based at home no longer than four or five months. It happened *so* quickly that I didn't have time to think about the mission or the purpose of the company, or the value of planning.

I sent a range of five or six products to one of the chains: they added them to a selection of foods that were being blind-tested by a taste panel and I received a call the next day to say my dishes were the best. I wasn't surprised by the outcome, but I *was* absolutely delighted.

Then we had to make a very big decision. Should we tell our potential customer, our *new* customer, the truth, the *whole* truth: that we didn't have a factory? Or should we keep quiet and just work to find a solution? I believe that in life, whether in your personal or your business life, if you are open and honest, people will help you along. We took a huge risk and told the truth. There were a lot of people in that room. They listened to what we had to say and took stock. A company that they had just selected to give big business to didn't even have a factory. I was still working from home. Fortunately, they appreciated my openness and frankness. Very quickly we managed to hire a tiny unit and started producing finger foods from there. Business continued to increase every day, every week, so we decided to go into the recipe-dish market too.

To cut the story short, in order to raise finance we joined hands with an established company that was riding quite high at the time: they invested in the factory. We built our first unit and started producing recipe dishes in 1989. In the first week I think we produced 5000 meals; I was absolutely thrilled. Now we have two factories on the Derby site; we produce about 1.5 million meals a week and employ 800 people.

I have a big vision for this company. I would like to see it doubling or tripling in size, and I want to diversify into other types of food. We have already ventured into American foods; soon we will be launching other European foods as well. My long-term aim is to see my food being enjoyed worldwide.

Perween Warsi

Founder and Chief Executive Officer, *S&A Foods*

Passion

Including everybody ensures that each person comes to understand the high standard of quality that's expected from us as a supplier.

It's very important to have a passion for your business, a passion for the products you sell, to be proud of your business and for your people to be proud of what they are producing (in our case, good-quality food). They need to have confidence in themselves, knowing that they are doing the job well. People matter because the business is not the bricks and mortar; the business is the people.

We hold taste panels every day before each product is released; I get involved personally on the Tuesday morning panel because I am passionate about maintaining quality. We invite a cross-section of people from across the company, including food preparation people, our cooks, people from the filling room, line setters, the departmental managers... everybody. Including everybody ensures that each person comes to understand the high standard of quality that's expected from us as a supplier and why we want to be proud of selling our products. You can tell from the way people talk that they have a passion for what they do. If you encourage that understanding in people, you don't need to tell them what to do because they will already have done it.

On one occasion we were expecting a visit from a customer. I found out about it at four-thirty or five o'clock on the previous day. I rang my chef: 'We have this customer visit, what are we going to do about it? What are we sampling?' The kitchen had prepared for the visit, but they had not prepared the things that I felt we should be sampling. I had a chat with him and said: 'Look, this is a good opportunity for us and we should be sampling this, that and the other.' He could tell how passionate I was about it; I really wanted to excite my customers. His response was: 'If I have to come in at five in the morning to prepare those products, I'll do it. Leave it to me and I'll sort it out.' The customer visit was at ten o'clock the next morning. When I went into the development kitchen, I found the entire table laid out with a fantastic range of food. The chef had gone to such trouble because he believed that it was very important to do so, and he was proud to do the work.

When I first set up the business I had five women helping me; it was a very easy process to manage because we talked to each other. When you have 800 people working in the business, communication becomes extremely difficult. I can't achieve my vision on my own; I need every single one of my management team to share the same passion, and then to convey that passion to everybody else on the factory floor. If you win hearts and minds, if you train people, if you develop them, if you give them the confidence to feel good about what they do, then the magic happens. The passionate approach works because you're dealing with people.

1986	**S&A Foods**
	Founder and Chief Executive Officer
	Founded company making Indian foodstuffs, and won first major contract to supply chilled and frozen dishes to Asda and Safeway stores.
1989	First factory built in Derby, creating over 100 jobs for the area.
1996	New bespoke factory built next to the original site.

Investing time and energy in an individual's development reaps dividends of increased loyalty and motivation. Developing people beyond their existing capabilities by involving them in more facets of the business can be extremely beneficial and is a company's responsibility.

4a **Trust, Develop, Stretch**
Stephen Dando

Director, BBC People, *BBC*

My Career

I've worked in a number of different business sectors during my career: car manufacturing; electronics; consumer products in the drinks industry, and for the last couple of years in the BBC. My career has been both domestically and internationally focused. In the last ten years or so I've spent a lot of time working across the world in different environments – in North America, Latin America, the Far East and in Europe.

I've got a lot of experience as a human resources (HR) generalist, and have also worked in specialist areas, the major one being people development. I've held corporate roles at the centre of organizations, as well as roles in operating companies away from the centre. It's been a varied career – although most HR people will tell you that the similarities between sectors are greater than the differences.

Stephen Dando

Director of BBC People, *BBC*

Trust, Develop, Stretch

My first experience after leaving university was gained in a small foundry in the Black Country in the Midlands. I was working at the time for Austin Rover, a car manufacturer, and I was sent to the foundry. I reported to an individual called the Personnel Manager, who was responsible for all the people issues in this foundry. 'What a great job,' I thought. Personnel work was what I wanted to do at some stage, and he clearly had loads of experience.

The manager was well on in his career, but I quickly realized that I'd been imposed on him by head office. He had no concept of his responsibility for developing me. If you're a graduate trainee working in human resources, the most exciting thing that can happen on a manufacturing site is to be in a position to observe when the convener of shop stewards comes into the room looking very upset and wanting to talk about an issue – and this would happen fairly regularly. However, on these occasions my boss would just look across to my corner of the room and gesture at me with his thumb to indicate that it was time for me to leave. It was made quite clear that whenever there was anything remotely exciting going on I had to leave the room. Of course, I felt acutely that experiences from which I could learn a great deal were being denied to me.

I later moved to Longbridge, Austin Rover's biggest manufacturing site at the time, and certainly one of the biggest in Europe. There I worked for someone in industrial relations who was a complete inspiration. His approach was diametrically different from that of my former boss. If a situation was developing that he thought would be useful learning for me, he'd put the thing on hold, go and find me, and get me involved. He was actively trying to bring me into important experiences. At the end of key meetings with unions and other officials he would always find five minutes to tell me what was really going on, and to make sure that I'd drawn the right understanding or inference or learning from the experience.

If a situation was developing that he thought would be useful learning for me, he'd put the thing on hold; he'd go and find me, and he'd get me involved. He was actively trying to bring me into important experiences.

He taught me to be true to the principle of first making sure that you get great people in place – there is no substitute for that – but then really stretching them. Give them opportunities – whether by appointing them to a job that's just slightly ahead of their current level of experience, or by creating a challenge that really stretches them. I've found that if you invest in someone's development, and you demonstrate trust and confidence in them, they will invariably pay you back with interest.

By the time I joined United Distillers in the late 1980s I'd reached a point in my career where I had a lot of experience of industrial relations and in what we would call generalist HR work, and I had a real interest in training and development. United Distillers was the spirits arm of what was then Guinness plc. The HR Director had recruited me to undertake training and development across thirty or forty sites in Scotland, but I had no great expertise in that field; in fact, some would say I was very limited in that area. The HR Director regarded that as a positive advantage because he wanted to challenge and change a lot of the old thinking about how people were trained and developed. He felt I'd be able to draw on my general experience and my interest in the subject to make a real impact. He took a big punt on me, but believed in my ability to do the job. I felt hugely indebted to him because it was a field I wanted to break into and he was prepared to trust me. I can recall feeling highly motivated to demonstrate to him that he'd made the right decision.

I've found that if you invest in someone's development, and you demonstrate trust and confidence in them, they will invariably pay you back with interest.

His approach reinforced for me the point that if you think you've got the right person, it's worth sometimes just really having a go and stretching them beyond their existing capabilities. You'll often be pleasantly surprised at what you get back.

Investing time
and money in
team development
significantly enhances
the team's overall
effectiveness.
Developing the right
dynamic between team
players encourages
high performance,
better understanding
and shared learning.

4b   **Teamwork**

If one can get the dynamics of a team right, its effectiveness can be enhanced significantly. It's an outcome that organizations have to invest in to get right, but it's worth the time, and sometimes money, to achieve the ensuing benefits.

Most people spend a great deal of their life working in teams, and if a team works well, it's quite clear that the organization is going to get a lot more from the people in it, and a better contribution to the company over time. I've worked in many teams during my career, and I've also had responsibility for leading teams. The insight I've gained over that time is that the whole really is greater than the sum of the parts. If one can get the dynamics of a team right, its effectiveness can be enhanced significantly. It's an outcome that organizations have to invest in to get right, but it's worth the time, and sometimes money, to achieve the ensuing benefits.

When I joined the Board of Guinness a few years ago I was joining a team that had invested quite a lot in its own development over a period of time. The experience of belonging to a high-performing team that had got to grips with issues surrounding such matters as the relationships within the group was very impressive. The team had learnt to deal with issues and make decisions in a way that enabled it to move forward. The experience reinforced my belief that working to develop teams really pays back in a big way.

What really makes the difference in effective teams is deepening relationships and the understanding that individuals have of each other. The process of achieving that reinforces the shared view of what they are there to achieve within the company, and the result will be a much stronger common view about how to achieve those outcomes. It's the understanding and awareness of who we are as individuals that allows teams to work together more effectively. The company also learns about the individuals who are sitting around the table.

I t's the understanding and awareness of who we are as individuals that allows teams to work together more effectively.

My experience has made me realize that usually there is not a great deal of understanding within the team about who each person is as an individual, and therefore it's not surprising that they come up against a lot of issues they find quite difficult to deal with. Teams nowadays have very heavy agendas, with so many priorities and issues to deal with that to spend time looking at how they work together would feel like an indulgence. There is a sense that team development is something you do only when you've completed everything else – and of course that moment never arrives. It's counter-intuitive in some ways; because most teams are under a fair bit of pressure, their instinct is to get on with the work in hand, but improving team effectiveness makes the work in hand that much easier.

Teams nowadays have very heavy agendas, with so many priorities and issues to deal with that to spend time looking at how they work together would feel like an indulgence.

During 2004 at the BBC we made a big investment of time in team development. Occasionally some of the team wondered whether we shouldn't be spending more time on the task, and less working on our own development, but overall I think we've all seen real benefits. It's important to integrate the organization's development activity with the work of the team as much as possible. Therefore when time is carved out specifically for development – such as an away-day – we also dedicate a proportion of the time we have available to focus on team development. One of the benefits of this approach is that the team developmental value is still very fresh for people, and can be more readily applied if they are getting on with real work as part of the same event.

It's important to integrate the development activity with the work of the team as much as possible.

My last employer, Diageo, did a lot of team development activity at various different levels. The executive committee saw it as a high priority and invested significant time in looking at team effectiveness. I don't think there's any doubt that the issues teams face have a real bearing on the success and the effectiveness of organizations generally. Team development is not a commitment that very commercially focused people would make if they didn't think there was a pretty obvious return on their investment. 99

	Degree in business law and administration, University of Strathclyde
	MBA, University of Edinburgh
1984	**Austin Rover**
	Graduate Trainee
1985–1989	**Ferranti International**
	Ferranti International supplies advanced systems to markets in business, defence and the community around the world.
1989–1997	**United Distillers**
	United Distillers was the spirits business of Guinness.
1997–1999	**Diageo**
	Diageo was formed in December 1997 through the merger of GrandMet and Guinness. At the time of the merger Diageo was a broad-based consumer goods company, with food and drinks at its core.
1999–2000	**UDV Europe (United Distillers & Vintners)**
	UDV Europe was created from the integration of IDV and UD, the spirits businesses of Grand Met and Guinness.
2000–2001	**Guinness**
	Global Human Resources Director
2001–2004	**British Broadcasting Corporation (BBC)**
	Director of Human Resources and Internal Communications
2004–present	*Director, BBC People*
	Change of job title reflected the new name of that BBC division.
	Member, BBC's Executive Board.

Never underestimate
the innate talent or
ambition of your people
Unlock their potential
by encouraging them
to think outside their
traditional boundaries,
as Pearson did when
printers were retrained
as journalists at the
Financial Times.

5a **Unlocking Potential**
Sir David Bell

Director for People, *Pearson;* Chairman, *Financial Times Group*

My Career

I've got two jobs: one as Chairman of the Financial Times (FT) Group, and the other being responsible for all the people within Pearson plc. We have about 30,000 people spread over fifty-one countries, the majority being in the United States. I have this rather funny title of Director for People; we chose the title because it matched the existing title of the Director for Finance.

I don't much like the words 'human resources' and 'personnel' if they are used in a way that implies 'units'. Our starting point is that people have to be seen as individuals, particularly in a creative business like ours. I chose my title and then found that Southwest Airlines in the USA also used it, so I flew with them to try to find out what it was that made them special. I couldn't completely work it out because they seemed to be throwing peanuts up and down the aisle.

My primary job is being responsible for all the people in the company. I used to run the *Financial Times* and I'm still the Chairman of the FT Group, so it's a dual role.

Sir David Bell

Director for People, *Pearson*; Chairman, *Financial Times Group*

We were faced with a situation where hundreds were going to lose their jobs, so we decided to offer as many as wanted it the chance to retrain as journalists.

While I was working at the *Financial Times*, we took the decision to close our printing plant. The decision was to affect a lot of people who had been with us a long time. We were faced with a situation where hundreds were going to lose their jobs, so we decided to offer as many as wanted it the chance to retrain as journalists. None had a single qualification between them. We developed a set of structured questions, put them to approximately thirty people, and offered training to eight of them. The process taught us that managers should never assume that people don't have ambition, or that they can't do anything more than they are already doing, or that they don't matter very much – because those assumptions are almost always wrong.

We gave our eight new trainees a six-month training programme in London. Three of them are still working for us ten years later, and the others left to become journalists elsewhere. These people had originally been separated by only 6 feet of concrete from the floor I had worked on as a journalist, yet they could have been on a different planet.

We were very proud of what our approach had achieved, and we've since developed the philosophy in a slightly different way. We've said to all 30,000 people in the business that we want to talk to them about how they're doing their present jobs and what they might do in the future. Most of them will say: 'I'm quite happy doing what I'm doing.' Few people are ambitious to do other things: if they were, it would be much harder to run a business. However, many more than you might think *have* got ideas about what they would like to do. We are convinced that this process will give us lots of leads regarding what people might do in the future, and whether they might need more training to achieve their aims.

W e believe that we have to structure the programme in a way that enables us to understand the kinds of things people would like to do...to enable us to unlock the talent in those who sometimes don't get heard and don't get asked.

There are those who say: 'Yours is a very dangerous philosophy. Just because you can play the piano doesn't mean you're going to end up being Chopin. Just because you can play golf doesn't mean you're going to end up being the next Tiger Woods.' We don't believe that's a reason for

We structure the programme very carefully so we don't raise expectations that we then can't meet.

not following it. We believe, on the contrary, that we have to structure the programme in a way that enables us to understand the kinds of things people would like to do; to see where and whether we can give them a chance to do those things; and to enable us to unlock the talent that may be there – talent in those who sometimes don't get heard and don't get asked. However, we do structure the programme very carefully so that we don't raise expectations that we then can't meet.

It doesn't matter what qualifications you have or lack; if you really want to do things in this business, you can. One of our most successful businesses is run by someone who left school at the age of sixteen. We have thousands of people working in warehouses in the United States and elsewhere doing quite repetitive jobs. I always think that some of those people, like our printers, will achieve great things if given the right opportunity. It's very important to us to send that signal

Don't just pay lip-service to listening to your people: make sure the reality matches the rhetoric, and encourage a flow of ideas between junior and senior management. By cultivating people's ambitions you will be repaid with hard work and loyalty.

Young Monks

People don't want to work *for* a company, they want to work *with* a company.

We wouldn't want a 'command and control' environment at Pearson; people don't want to work *for* a company, they want to work *with* a company. It is very important to distinguish between those two little words: 'for' and 'with'. My own aversion to the idea of working *for* a company may go back to my early career as a journalist – journalists hate command and control – but it's also because creative people don't respond to it. People want to feel that they're partners rather than employees in the workplace, so we try not to use the word 'employee'.

Business leaders need to learn to listen to what is happening within businesses in a way that perhaps they haven't listened before. They need to listen: but to listen and *hear*, not to listen and *not* hear. I remember once meeting someone from IBM who said he had an open-door policy for all staff. I said: 'Wow, that's fantastic.' He said: 'Yes, my door is open every Monday from 9.15 to 9.30.' Well, what we want within our organization is the opposite of that attitude; that means managers need to listen, they need to be *seen* to be listening, and, importantly, they need to *mean* that they are listening.

St Benedict's rule was always to listen to the young monks, because they know all the things you've forgotten.

Marjorie Scardino, the Chief Executive of Pearson, sends out a series of emails, which are called 'Dear Everyone' letters. She gets an average of 900 replies to each and she replies to them all: these are a good way of listening. Each year the company arranges for 120 of the newest, most junior managers to spend three days together with the very top echelon of management. They have the opportunity to talk about the future, about the challenges facing the company, what they've already learned, what they would like to do, and the skills they might need to end up running the company one day. This practice enables the Directors to understand what's going on in the company and, best of all, to understand the way we do things.

St Benedict founded the Benedictine order in the sixth century, so it has now been running a lot longer than any corporation. His rule was always to listen to the young monks because they know all the things you've forgotten. By and large we find that rule to be true. Pearson's business is newspapers and book publishing: in fact, we're the biggest book publisher in the world, the biggest educational publisher in the world. The only asset we have is the people who create our newspapers, our magazines and our books. We have no other assets. Therefore, being connected and close to our people offers a constant reminder that our business is not about computers or buildings or anything other than people. All businesses are like that, but creative businesses particularly so.

We measure our success first of all by how many of our people are the best in the business and how many we keep: we are pretty happy about that because we do quite well on that score. Second, we measure whether or not we are developing skills that we can move across the business. We have a long way to go in that regard, but we're doing better than we did. Finally, we undertake satisfaction surveys to try to find out whether people like working for us and whether they think the company offers them real opportunities for the future.

We feel that we are in a contract with the people who work for us. Our side of the contract is to give them an opportunity, to give them training, to give them real potential for the future: their side of the contract is to work as hard as they possibly can with us. If we both keep our side of the contract, we're going continue to have a great business.

People are integral to an organization, so taking their personal lives and issues into consideration should be common practice. Doing so fosters better working relationships and a higher commitment to the company.

The Way We Work

If managers and leaders take time to understand the issues that are confronting people, they will work better, the company will work better, and in the end their commitment to the company is going to be higher.

It is easy to forget that the people who come to work don't exist just in the workplace: they have other lives; they are whole people. If an organization forgets that, it does so at its peril.

One of the important things that we strive to do at Pearson is to take account of the need for work/life balance – not in what could be called a soft way, but because it is a good investment. If managers and leaders take time to understand the issues that are confronting people, they will work better, the company will work better, and in the end their commitment to the company is going to be higher.

You would not have found such an approach in this company fifty years ago. I met an elderly woman the other day who had been secretary to Lord Cowdray, one of the Directors years ago. A colleague of hers, a man with a child, had asked one Christmas whether he could have Boxing Day off as well as Christmas Day. His boss had refused and, at the time, that attitude was not considered unreasonable. So in terms of corporate culture we've come a long way over the years.

At the point I joined the *Financial Times* as Advertisement Director we employed no women at all in the senior jobs. During the time I was there I promoted a lot of women. An incident occurred one day: a woman – a mother – had asked whether she could go home to look after her child, who was ill. The man for whom she worked refused permission, saying: 'You came here to work and you can wait until the end of the day.' I brought all the managers into my office and said that if such a thing ever happened again, the culprit who had said 'No' would be fired. I think this astonished them but it never did happen again. The only reason the men in that room did not have the same issues to contend with was that they had partners at home looking after their children for them; once you accept that fact, the idea of striking a balance in the workplace becomes easier.

You have to assume that the people who work for you are not trying to slide out and avoid working. They're not making excuses. It is very, very rare for somebody to be dishonest about needing to go home to look after his or her child. If we begin with the assumption that the person who has asked is being honest, we believe them. If people are believed, and they have a supportive manager, they are going to be much more effective – once they have been able to deal with the problem – than if they are sitting at their desk worrying about it.

We employ more women than we do men, which has forced us to look at this issue closely. But unequal numbers isn't the only reason for looking into this: it is also a question of fundamental fairness. Another problem that is increasingly relevant relates not so much to looking after children as to the issues surrounding the care of elderly relatives. We offer a service – an employee helpline – that gives advice and can suggest places to go for further help and so on. We offer a lot of benefits like that and they are very popular.

As a company we are going to become more flexible about working hours, particularly around school holidays because sometimes people need to be at home then. We are going to start thinking about people working a number of hours across a whole year, rather than across a week or a month. We are going to be more balanced, more flexible – but I doubt that we will ever see a situation where our best editor will be editing books for us while sitting in southern Italy. I don't think that's going to work because people need to be together.

It is my belief that we are never going to have a situation where people will be working from home all the time. The idea that people can be in a creative business and do everything from home is not going to work. It is conceivable that people will spend a greater proportion of their time working at home than they do currently, but we find that bringing people together is very important to maintain the spark of creativity.

Executive Timeline Sir David Bell

1970	**_Oxford Mail and Times_**
	Reporter
1972	**_Financial Times_**
	Washington Correspondent
	News Editor
	Worked on the launch of the International Edition
	Features Editor
	Managing Editor
	Advertisement Director
1993	**Financial Times Group**
	Chief Executive
1996	**Pearson Group**
	Director
	The Pearson Group is a global company that includes the Penguin Group, Pearson Education and the FT Group, and specializes in newspapers, trade publishing and education, including assessment and testing.
1996–present	**Financial Times Group**
	Chairman
	Personally spearheaded the FT Group's expansion into Asia.
1998–present	**Pearson**
	Director for People
	Responsible for the recruitment, motivation, development and reward of all employees.
2004	Awarded a knighthood for his contribution to the world of journalism and communication, and his work with the homeless and disadvantaged.

The 'soft' option is never an option, as ignoring a problem and hoping it will go away just makes things worse. Direct, candid feedback at the time is essential; people deserve that honesty, and are likely to thrive as a result.

6   **Always Deliver Honest Feedback**
Amelia Fawcett

Vice Chairman, *Morgan Stanley International*

My Career

I have had an interesting career and one that is not particularly traditional for an investment banker. After university I worked in New York as a paralegal because I had always wanted to be a lawyer – and, indeed, I did become a lawyer. I went to law school at the University of Virginia, and upon graduation moved to New York in the early 1980s to work at a major New York firm, Sullivan & Cromwell. There I focused mainly on banking, mergers and acquisitions and underwriting work. It was a very interesting time to be in New York – the beginning of the era of large international deals, large mergers and acquisitions transactions, and the growth of the financial services business generally.

Towards the end of 1985, Sullivan & Cromwell asked me to go and work in the firm's Paris office. I was very 'disappointed', since I really wanted to live and work in London. However, I was told that, since I spoke French, I was going to go to Paris. After the vibrancy and fast pace of New York, it was a very different place to be – there was not much going on in Financial Services, little public mergers and acquisitions work (much less 'hostile' deals) and the financial markets were rather sleepy – so very different from the Paris financial markets of today! I wondered what I was doing there, but in the end it was a great experience because I did so many different things.

I moved to Morgan Stanley in early 1987 to help set up a Legal and Compliance department. In the early days I focused very much on investment banking, mergers and acquisitions. I advised on the legal and operational sides of deals but gradually began doing more work on the sales and trading side (including derivatives and commodities), as well as being part of the team that opened offices in many countries. I think I have worked (in some capacity) on the opening or establishment of almost every Morgan Stanley office outside the United States, with the exception of Tokyo and Hong Kong. The experience allowed me to work with a variety of people who were building new businesses and looking for people who could help them 'execute' on business plans. So I was asked to come out of the legal department and work for the joint CEOs.

My Europe-wide remit was to work on 1) helping build businesses with governments, as well as policy initiatives with governments, 2) developing a media and communications strategy, and 3) developing community/CSR strategy led by senior management and 4) – as the firm really began to focus on strategic initiatives – to set up a strategy function, then an operational risk function.

I became Chief Administrative Officer and Managing Director in 1996 and Vice Chairman of Morgan Stanley in 2002. In addition I have done a lot of work, which I very much enjoy, outside the firm. Until recently, I was Deputy Chairman of the National Employment Panel. Now I am a member of the Court of the Bank of England, a trustee of the National Portrait Gallery, the Chairman of the London International Festival Theatre, a member of the Governing Council of the University of London and a Trustee of the National Maritime Museum (Cornwall), to name a few.

Amelia Fawcett

Vice Chairman, *Morgan Stanley International*

Always Deliver Honest Feedback

I think one of the most important, but often one of the hardest, lessons that we need to learn as managers is how to deliver honest feedback. When I was a youngish manager, the company hired a young Vice President to join us from another firm. It was a more star-orientated firm than ours where we were very focused on teamwork – working together to push the franchise and the interests of the client forward.

In his early days in the firm the newcomer kept putting himself in front of the team, putting himself centre stage in front of the firm, and in front of the Press. It was clear that the Press were not interested in him *per se*, and it wasn't in the interests of the firm to have him out there on his own. He had committed what was a cardinal sin at Morgan Stanley, in focusing on himself to the exclusion of others. In a firm such as ours, as in many others, the team orientation to work together and push together for the client is critical – so critical that when the Press call up and say: 'We'd like to speak to your banker who did the "xyz" deal,' we say: 'Well, it wasn't a banker, it was a team.' 'Could we have a photograph of the banker?' 'It wasn't a banker, it was a team... If you want a photograph, we could give you a team photograph.'

This individual had acted in a way that was completely contrary to our ethos and it was disruptive to the team, difficult for the franchise, and sent a very bad message to the people who worked for him. With an issue like that, if you don't tackle it very early it can become divisive. It was clear to me that I had several options: I could let it go until the end of the year and give him the feedback in his annual review; I could ignore it and hope it went away or that he'd pick up the 'problem' by osmosis; or I could deal with it directly.

As I was a young manager and this was clearly going to be an uncomfortable meeting and was not something I really wanted to do, I went to talk to the CEO. We talked it through and he said: 'It's a serious issue: it's about culture, it's about how you work with other people, and it's going to have a divisive impact, given where he sits with other people. We need to deal with it now.'

We pulled our colleague in and told him in a straightforward, honest, direct, aggressive, but constructively critical way that he was behaving in a manner that was contrary to the culture and the interests of the firm, that he had six weeks to show significant progress, and that if he didn't make significant progress, we would ask him to leave the firm. It was a very uncomfortable meeting for all three of us. I'm delighted to say that he took the criticism on board, he worked on it immediately and became very much a team player. He has gone on to be successively promoted, and is a terrific team player within the firm.

The most difficult question for all managers is how best to manage our people. There is often the temptation to think: 'Wouldn't it be easier to sugar-coat the message?' The lesson for me is that the 'soft' option is never an option. It's not fair to the individual concerned; it's not fair to the firm and its clients. If a manager is direct and candid, he is actually doing a great deal of good and is being very honest with his colleagues. I think a lot of people believe that trouble will simply go away, but in my experience a difficult problem never goes away. It probably increases in intensity and becomes much worse and therefore much harder to deal with. It was a very useful lesson for me, albeit a difficult one, that honesty and candour are the fairer options. They are good for the person or people concerned, and good for the firm.

There is often the temptation to think: 'Wouldn't it be easier to sugar-coat the message?' The lesson for me is that the 'soft' option is never an option. It's not fair to the individual concerned; it's not fair to the firm and its clients.

When you're having a conversation with an individual who is experiencing difficulties you need to be very clear as to what the issues are. You need to be very supportive and constructively critical, but at the end of the day neither you nor the individual concerned can be under any misunderstanding as to what has been said, what is required

A lot of people believe that trouble will simply go away, but in my experience a difficult problem never goes away. It probably increases in intensity and becomes much worse and therefore much harder to deal with.

from both parties, and what will happen if either party doesn't deliver what it's supposed to. People look for stability, honesty and a certain measure of loyalty. I think being candid and giving people honest feedback is loyal to them as well as loyal to the firm.

Executive Timeline Amelia Fawcett

1974–1978	Degree in history, Wellesley College, USA.
1978–1980	**Sullivan & Cromwell** *Paralegal* Major New York law firm
1980–1983	University of Virginia School of Law (JD)
1983–1986	**Sullivan & Cromwell** *Lawyer* Worked in New York and Paris.
1987	**Morgan Stanley** Joined the London office of this large, international financial services firm. She has since been with the firm, and in London, for more than 18 years.
1990	*Vice President*
1992	*Executive Director*
1996	*Managing Director and Chief Administrative Officer for the European operations*
2002–present	**Morgan Stanley International** *Vice Chairman*

A good manager tackles problems head-on and acts decisively, without hesitation – even when faced with tough personnel issues.

7 **Be Tough but Compassionate**
Peter Ellwood

Chairman, *ICI*; former Group Chief Executive, *Lloyds TSB Group*

My Career

My career started when I was fifteen and still at school, as the result of my Careers Master asking whether I would like to see how a bank runs. I said: 'Sure,' and went on a three-day programme to Lloyds Bank Training Centre in Hindhead, Surrey. They said: 'This is how a bank works: and, by the way, next week we're taking you to see the head office of Lloyds Bank at 71 Lombard Street in London.'

When we arrived we were shown the strongroom, where our guide told us: 'This door weighs 10 tons — and yet you can move it with a single finger.' He noticed me and said: 'Hey, you, come and move it.' I did move it — and with a single finger because this enormous door was so well balanced. I decided immediately that I wanted to work in the banking industry. I decided to become a banker.

When I left school I joined Barclays Bank rather than Lloyds because it had a decentralized approach. I stayed there for about twenty years, left to join the Trustee Savings Bank (TSB) and ran that for several years. I then decided that TSB could not survive on its own, and instigated the sale of it to Lloyds. I ran Lloyds TSB for seven years as Chief Executive, and have been Chairman at ICI since 2004.

The beauty of the story is that when I became Chief Executive of Lloyds TSB I was based at 71 Lombard Street — the building that housed the strongroom I had visited when I was fifteen years old.

Peter Ellwood

Chairman, *ICI*; former Group Chief Executive, *Lloyds TSB Group*

Be Tough but Compassionate

If he knows he has to act, the good manager will always grasp the nettle and take the action, but will do it with sensitivity and with compassion.

It is very important that a manager is able to be tough, while at the same time being compassionate. I once made the mistake of trying to be compassionate at the expense of being tough, which confused the issue.

In the 1990s I was Chief Executive of the TSB banking group. I had to manage a fellow member of the Board who was very senior, and who had worked for the company for thirty years. He'd given his job a really good shot and he wasn't doing it badly, but he wasn't really performing and his numbers weren't coming through. I needed to have somebody in place who could do the job brilliantly.

I met with him on a regular basis: he asked me questions that he should have been able to answer, or asked me to make decisions that frankly he should have been making himself. When I asked him about his business, he didn't know the answers as well as he should. In fact, I began to know more about his business than he did – and that's when I started to get worried.

I decided to try to offer him a lesser job. It was still quite an important job, but it was a lesser job nevertheless, and he prevaricated for about a month. In the end I told him that we needed to know whether or not he was going to take it. By then I had allowed him to create negativity within the organization because clearly he was not happy. I spoke to him one evening and said: 'Look, this is not going to work; you are going to have to go. Why don't we say the story is that you have elected to go because you want to do other things?' This allowed him to spin the story that he was leaving of his own volition. So in the end I got tough and he went, but I had still treated him compassionately. Since then I have not given people the luxury of an alternative option. If I have thought that they should go, then they've gone and they've gone quickly.

Don't fudge matters. Don't assume that problems might go away. It is an emotional as well as a mental issue: if you know in your heart that somebody is not right for the job, that somebody else could do that job better, more effectively, and could be world class, you have to act. You owe it to yourself, you owe it to your team – and ultimately you owe it to your shareholders.

When my direct reports come to see me for their formal session each month, they talk about their people. If they don't raise issues about their people and how they've got on over the previous four weeks, I will ask questions because the most

I't's important that a manager
lives in the real world and does not
pretend that things will always turn
out well.

important thing a manager has to do is manage other people.
When they say: 'We're thinking about Bert; he's not doing
terribly well, but I think he'll be all right,' I say: 'Well, you told
me that Bert wasn't doing terribly well two months ago. How
long are you going to give him?' If the manager then says: 'I'm
working on him,' I will suggest that we should decide there
and then that if he's not doing well within an agreed period
of time, he's out. By that method I help managers crystallize
their own thoughts about their people. It's important that
a manager lives in the real world and does not pretend that
things will always turn out well. If he knows he has to act, the
good manager will always grasp the nettle and take the action
but will do it with sensitivity and compassion. 99

Executive Timeline Peter Ellwood

1961–1985	**Barclays Bank**
	Various roles in retail and corporate banking.
1985–1989	**Barclaycard**
	Chief Executive
	This part of Barclays Bank was one of the largest credit card companies in the world at that time.
1989–1995	**TSB Group**
1989	*Chief Executive – Retail Banking*
1990	*Chief Executive – Retail Banking & Insurance*
1992	*Group Chief Executive*
1995	TSB Group merged with Lloyds to become one of the largest forces in domestic banking in the UK.
1996–2003	**Lloyds TSB**
1996	*Deputy Group Chief Executive*
1997–2003	*Group Chief Executive*
2003–present	**Imperial Chemical Industries (ICI)**
2003	*Deputy Chairman*
2004–present	*Chairman*
	ICI is one of the world's largest producers of speciality products and paints.

Occasionally focusing on detail is important as it helps to monitor decisions being taken, and the organization is kept on its toes if it knows this dive into detail could happen at any time.

8a **The Benefits of Micromanagement**
Dawn Airey

Managing Director: Sky Networks, *British Sky Broadcasting Group*

My Career

I graduated from Cambridge in 1984 and went straight to Central Television as a graduate trainee. It was an incredible production powerhouse in the 1980s. At the end of my two years' training I started a programming career in light entertainment. I was an Associate Producer on shows such as *Classmates*; a Researcher on *Blockbusters*, *The Price Is Right*, *The $64,000 Question* – all high-quality, long-running entertainment series. What I really wanted to do, though, was to be a Producer in the News and Current Affairs department. My boss used to ask me every six months: 'What do you want to do, Dawn?' I would say: 'I want to be a Producer in the Current Affairs department.' And he would say: 'No, I think you're Entertainment.' He would always give me things to do other than what I really wanted to do. One day he said: 'I think you could be a Scheduler. You're always saying to me: "That's in the wrong place" and "Why on earth did somebody do that?"'

At the time, ITV's schedule was compiled by the big five companies. They got together every other week and carved up the schedule between them. Central Television's planner, a wonderful man called John Terry, was about to retire. I told my boss: 'No, I don't want to be a Scheduler. I want eventually to be a Controller of factual programmes, but a Producer in the short term.' My boss said: 'Well, I'll double your salary, and give you a company car.' The car was the clincher, so I said: 'Fine.' For an XR2, I became a Scheduler of Central for a couple of years, and because I was good at that, I was also asked to run the press office and the presentation department and research. So at the end of the day I was Director of Broadcasting. I was at Central for a total of eight years, but did something new every couple of years.

The ITV Network Centre was established in response to the 1990 Broadcasting Act, which said ITV had to have a separate commissioning and scheduling body. I was recruited as Controller of Children's and Daytime TV. I held the post for two years, and it proved to be a calling card to become Controller of Arts and Entertainment at Channel 4, where I led a team that commissioned everything from *Father Ted* to *Brass Eye*, and acquired *Friends* and *ER*. These were halcyon days, a really fantastic and creative period in Channel 4's history. From Channel 4 I went to Channel 5 – another happy accident.

My career has been a series of happy accidents. I received a phone call from Greg Dyke to say there were four bids going in for Channel 5, and the consortium he was involved in wanted me to be Director of Programmes. I held that post for five years, became Chief Executive for two years, and was then in the lovely position of ITV wanting me to be their Chief Executive. Sky made a very audacious bid on the day I was about to sign for ITV and invited me to become Managing Director of Sky Networks. I thought: 'I don't know much about multi-channel telly, but I need to go to Sky because that is where the bigger challenge is going to be.' And I was right!

Dawn Airey

Managing Director: Sky Networks, *British Sky Broadcasting Group*

The Benefits of Micromanagement

Micromanagement is a highly undervalued aspect of the manager's strategic armoury. You're in a senior position and there to take an overview of the department or team: to give guidance, to sort out problems. In the main you should let those people who report to you just get on and deal with the day-to-day detail, but it's absolutely vital and totally invaluable occasionally to dive into particular issues, first to understand the detailed dynamics of what is going on, and also to keep everybody on their toes.

My experience has been primarily in a creative industry, where I've been responsible for schedules and running creative organizations with creative individuals. Now effective scheduling is absolutely critical when you're a broadcaster. You're transmitting twenty-four hours a day, so what appears at what time, what the legacy is, or what is going on on other channels can often be as important as the quality of the show. If you get any of that wrong – if you place your crown jewel against *Coronation Street*, for example – it's very unlikely that it's going to be adequately sampled. Therefore, what I've done throughout my career when I've been leading networks, or teams of networks, is to focus occasionally on a weekly, daily, or quarterly scheduling period, and take time to understand the dynamics of what is going on.

For example, when I was in charge of children's programmes and daytime programmes for ITV, I worked alongside a scheduler. We used to dive into the detail and absolutely understand it – to the extent that we could predict with

W hat I've done throughout my career when I've been leading networks, or teams of networks, is to focus occasionally on a weekly, daily, or quarterly scheduling period, and really take time to understand the dynamics of what is going on.

alarming accuracy what the BBC (because it was very predictable) was going to do on which nights. You could almost guarantee the week's numbers, because they'd never had opposition before. The team wasn't used to somebody micromanaging and analysing the detail. We did that to great advantage because we knew what to avoid and, equally, knew where to put our strong programmes up against the opposition's. The system worked well.

At Sky One scheduling is even more interesting than scheduling terrestrial channels. Sky One is among over seventy channels in my portfolio. As a multichannel, general entertainment channel available primarily through the digibox it will usually be accessed via only one television in the home. So if you've got a brilliant new drama or factual series to launch, there's absolutely no point in pitching it against Premier League football on a Monday night. Interestingly, the ownership of the remote control in most homes is a man, and more men like football than don't. You don't therefore put male-appeal titles against Premier League. Now that might sound really obvious, but the schedulers hadn't always considered these issues. So rather than think holistically about what's going on in the family, we just looked at the schedule: at the bigger picture. *That* was micromanagement. *That* was going in and saying: 'Let's understand the dynamics of what is happening on this day in the home.' From that point you ignore the fact that you as an individual aren't necessarily going to be watching what Sky One puts up because you've got too many choices: you've just got to play to your strengths. Again, it's micromanagement. It's about thinking: 'What are the opportunities here that are being missed?' Often the great thing about delving into very specific detail is that things become clearer. You think that you can't see the wood for the trees, when in actual fact it's the other way around.

Often the great thing about delving into very specific detail is that things become clearer.

There are times when you can't see the strikingly obvious, so something that I do from time to time is ask to be taken through the day: I ask for an explanation on every decision behind the schedule construction. Invariably, you can add something to it. It's not about continually going into detail: it's about an occasional dipstick that acts as a measure and shows the competence of the organization. It also reinforces the leader's position – demonstrating that actually they have

Going into detail is an occasional dipstick that acts as a measure and shows the competence of the organization.

something to add – and it also engages them in the detail. This makes the leader become a less remote figure in terms of running the business. However, it should be an occasional thing because people can predict when it will happen if it's too frequent. Far better to keep people on their toes and say: 'OK, we're going to look at this,' knowing that your interest might come out of the blue.

There will always be individuals who are difficult within an organization. These people need to be dealt with as soon as possible, clearly told what the rules of engagement are – and if the pain of dealing with them outweighs the gain, they have to go.

Dealing with High-maintenance Individuals

Dealing with High-maintenance Individuals

Most leaders will have to deal with high-maintenance
individuals at some point in their management career. I starte
out at Channel 4 as Controller of Arts and Entertainment,
plucked from relative obscurity: I was responsible for kids' an
daytime programming at ITV. Then one morning the Director
of Programmes, John Willis, said: 'Let's have breakfast, Dawn
Anybody who knows me well knows that I do not like getting
up early in the morning, so the idea of a breakfast meeting
was ghastly, but John said: 'It could be to your advantage.'
I thought: 'I really don't want breakfast.' Then he added:
'...breakfast at the Savoy.' I thought: 'Well, I've never had
breakfast at the Savoy, so I'll go.'

As I was walking over Waterloo Bridge towards the hotel, I
remembered that the Controller of Arts and Entertainment
for Channel 4 had just got a job as Managing Director of
Granada, so I thought: 'Oh, that's what he's going to ask me
about. He wants to talk to me about the job.' Fortunately, we
got on extremely well; I was offered the job and I took it.

Then there was a degree of outrage. Television, for all its
liberal nature and approach was quite white-collar and middl
class male in the early 1990s. It has improved tangibly over
the last five years, but I'm going back over ten years. From
nowhere, Channel 4, that mighty cultural institution, had
appointed somebody who didn't have great experience in arts
and entertainment, but who had a good track record of being

pretty commercial and shaking things up. I went to meet all my senior creative people and controllers. One individual, who shall remain nameless, came up to me after my first day and said: 'Well, I really don't like you. And actually, I really don't want you to be my boss. In fact, I don't think you're very good at all.' I said: 'That is very interesting and I really appreciate your candour because I'm going to be equally candid back. I know you are a very talented Commissioning Editor, but if the pain of working with you outweighs the gain – in fact, even if the pain equals the gain – I will have you out of this door immediately. And don't think I won't, because I will. I'm very happy to deal with you as a high-maintenance individual, but if that high maintenance is not equalled by over-delivery, you are out on your ear.'

Now the interesting thing is that we developed a very good relationship from then on because nobody had taken this individual on in such a candid way before. I was, in effect, saying: 'OK, that's fine, but I'm the boss and this is the way it's going to be.' And actually he responded rather well for it.

The lesson from that is: there are always individuals whom, when you put them together in a group, you are going to feel closer to. Likewise, there are always those who are going to be a little bit crotchety, or who will be nonconformist and come at things in a slightly different way. If they can be irritating, they will be. The reality is that if you work with a

The reality is that if you work with a group of people, you've got to embrace their differences.

group of people, you've got to embrace their differences but if somebody is out of kilter and becomes destructive within the team, or carries a really negative attitude for no reason other than they can, you just have to deal with it – head-on and as quickly as possible. Make it very clear what the rules of engagement are – and what the consequences are if they're breached. If the gain doesn't outweigh the pain, it's very simple: it's P45 time.

Executive Timeline Dawn Airey

1985	**Central TV**
	Management Trainee
	Associate Producer
1986	*Liaison Officer*
1988	*Controller of Programme Planning*
1989	*Director of Programme Planning*
1993	**ITV**
	Controller of Network Children's and Daytime Programmes
1994	**Channel 4**
	Controller of Arts and Entertainment
	Responsible for around 50 per cent of the channel's output.
	Channel 4 Television Corporation is a commercially funded television station owned by the UK government.
1996	**Channel 5 (now Five)**
	Director of Programmes
2000–2002	*Chief Executive*
2003–present	**British Sky Broadcasting (BSkyB)**
	Managing Director: Sky Networks
	Responsible for all wholly owned Sky Channels (with the exception of Sky Sports) and for Sky Media (airtime sales).
	BSkyB is the digital provider of pay-TV and joint owner of Freeview.

> There will always be people whose different personalities mean they don't see eye to eye. While you can't change this, helping them see each other's strengths will encourage them to work together more productively.

9

Keeping Peace Between People
Sir Mark Weinberg

President, *St James's Place Capital*

My Career

 I trained and worked originally as a lawyer, but in 1961 I went into business to form Abbey Life Assurance. I worked and built up that company for about eight years, and in 1970 it was bought out by ITT. The circumstances were such that I lost confidence in the shareholders, so I left. In 1971 I started a new company, originally called Hambro Life, but we changed its name subsequently to Allied Dunbar. This company was bought by BAT Industries in the mid-1980s, and in 1990 I left to start a new company called St James's Place.

Sir Mark Weinberg

President, *St James's Place Capital*

Marketing people and administrative people are very different from one another: they virtually come from different planets.

It's important to recognize that marketing people and administrative people are very different from one another: they virtually come from different planets. Marketing people tend to be optimistic and extrovert, while administrative production people are more likely to be disciplined and somewhat pessimistic, tending to spot problems that the marketing people don't see. These differences make it very difficult for them to work together; each group will blame the other if things are going slowly or not working.

I learnt a valuable lesson in how to manage these differences while running my first company, Abbey Life, about thirty years ago. I had a really first-rate Marketing Director and Administrative Director, and the company did very well as a result. However, if things went wrong, each of the Directors would spend a lot of time complaining about the other. In business, however good your administration, things do go wrong occasionally; however good your marketing, there will be times when the company has been over-optimistic with the sales forecasts, or when sales people are unreasonable in their expectations of the administrative team. I used to get the Administrative Director and the Marketing Director coming to my office separately and complaining about each other: 'We've got a very good marketing organization but the administration is ruining the business...;' 'It's all the Marketing Director's fault...' and so on.

I heard their long stories of woe on a regular basis. In response to this, I would call the two of them into my office once a month. They would sit there, usually feeling a bit uncomfortable with each other, while I spoke to each of them in turn. I would tell the Administrative Director that he was first rate, one of the best people in the business, and that he ran his section very efficiently. Then I would relate some of the good things that he'd done. I would turn to the Marketing Director and tell him how incredibly well he was doing too, what a good show he was putting on, how well he was doing relative to the competition, and so on. They would both start nodding. Then I would say: 'What we can't afford to have is friction between the marketing department and the administrative department. You have to work as a team: that's the only way things are going to work.'

At that point they would each start protesting that they hadn't been complaining about the other one, and they would go off arm in arm as if they were the greatest of colleagues.

Then I would close the door, take out my diary and note a date one month in the future on which to repeat the exercise, because I knew from experience it was bound to

You won't change the beast, but you've got to work at keeping peace between people and encourage them to see each other's strengths so that they will work together effectively.

happen again. You won't change the beast, but you've got to work at keeping peace between people and encourage them to see each other's strengths so that they will work together effectively. 99

Executive Timeline Sir Mark Weinberg

1961	**Abbey Life Assurance Company**
	Founding Director
	Founded Abbey Life Assurance Company in London, and formed one of the UK's first property funds.
1971	**Hambro Life Assurance** (now part of Zurich Financial Services)
	Founding Director
	Formed the first retail-managed fund.
	Hambro grew to become the largest unit-linked life assurance company in the UK. Later renamed Allied Dunbar.
1985–1990	**Securities and Investment Board**
	Deputy Chairman
	Held role from the Board's inception in 1985. It was the principal UK regulatory body.
1991	**St James's Place Capital**
	Co-founder and Chairman
	St James's Place is a wealth management group.
2004	*President*

Integrating companies after an acquisition is always a difficult process because if it is not done properly, an important part of what has been acquired can be lost. For success management must balance giving autonomy and respect with ensuring growth and profit.

10 **Integrating Cultures**
Maurice Levy

Chairman and Chief Executive Officer, *Publicis Groupe*

If I had to give advice to somebody joining an advertising agency, and Publicis in particular, I would probably recommend that the best way to grow is to work passionately, with total commitment to the agency and the client. I was working in another agency before I joined Publicis; I was twenty-nine years old and I was invited by my Chairman for lunch, face to face. He offered me the job of CEO of that agency. I laughed and said: 'I'm twenty-nine years old. CEO? I'm in the wrong agency, because this means that there is nobody here who is better than me.' So I left and I came to Publicis to start all over again with electronic data processing, what today we call IT.

I was fascinated by Publicis; fascinated by Marcel Bleustein-Blanchet, the founder, by his charm, his stories, his powerful personality – and I was lifted by the challenges we were faced with. I always wanted to impress Marcel. In French we say *épater*, which is to make totally astonished and overwhelmed by the success of an operation. He challenged me to see which level I could work to, instead of building my career in the conventional way by being first an Account Executive, then an Account Supervisor and then Vice-President, and so on. The reality is that you are judged by the passion that you put into the work you do, the passion and the commitment that you put into the relations you have with your clients, and how you build the growth of an agency. If you do that right, there is only one way to go, and that is up.

Maurice Levy

Chairman and Chief Executive Officer, *Publicis Groupe*

What unites Europe is its very diversity and its respect for individual cultural differences. This is something that is very, very important. The principles that apply to respecting cultural differences also apply when acquiring companies with differing corporate cultures.

Cultural diversity is something we touched upon at Publicis on the occasion of the single market in 1992, and at that time I tried to understand what was uniting Europe: what was all this about a single market? What made Europeans the same and what made them different? I categorized something like 500 commercials by humour, brand demonstration, gender differences, etc. A commercial that was considered to be very humorous in Germany, for example, would not be seen as funny in the UK or France. Similarly, the way a relationship between men and women was portrayed in some Italian commercials was considered absolutely unacceptable in France and the Nordic countries.

We are all European. We signed the European Treaty in 1958, but over 40 years later we are still very, very different – very attached to our individual culture, language and stories: and what is important to some is completely unimportant to others. What unites Europe is its very diversity and its respect for individual cultural differences. This is something that is very, very important. The principles that apply to respecting cultural differences also apply when acquiring companies with differing corporate cultures.

In our business, which is about communication, we need to connect with consumers if we want to bond with them. The only way to connect well is to use images, words and references that resonate with the consumer. To achieve this, we might refer to a global culture, such as music, or a very local culture that speaks to the minds and the hearts of the people.

When we started to acquire networks, such as Saatchi & Saatchi, Leo Burnett, Fallon and many other agencies, we had to face a very important problem: how could we protect the autonomy and identity of these agencies? We were buying the value of some clients and the co-operation of people who had worked in a certain environment. If we changed the environment too much, we would lose the people and/or the clients. Obviously, the best way to protect the environment is to offer maximum autonomy – but how do you give maximum autonomy and at the same time retain a certain level of control? As a shareholder, you not only retain a certain level of control, but you also need to gain acceptance from the people in order for them to be motivated to deliver growth, better profits and so on. The way we achieve that is first by respect. This word is very important. Respect for *la différence*.

The message we gave to our agency networks was: 'We are different. You are different. We want you to remain different because you are who you are. We respect your brand; we love it; that's the reason why we paid so much for it. We want you to continue to be who you are, but at the same time we want you to progress, and we want you to have total satisfaction in your job.'

We had a very important meeting at the beginning of the Saatchi & Saatchi acquisition. We went to Versailles, where we discussed what we would be doing in the future. Everyone agreed the master plan, but after a few weeks we saw that the Saatchi & Saatchi people were not really applying it. Some people at Publicis started to get nervous, and asked me to react strongly and perhaps show more clearly that *we* had acquired *them*. I spent some time thinking and said: 'That

The message we gave to our agency networks was: 'We are different. You are different. We want you to remain different because you are who you are.'

Respect sometimes works much better than money or tricks. When you are honest you have integrity and a genuine respect for people. They feel it, they understand it, and most of the time you have a natural bond that you can build upon.

would probably be a big mistake: rather, if we want to make it work, I must give them the feeling that *they* have bought *us*.' So instead I worked to make them feel that not only did we love them, respect them and value them, but also that they had bought us, and they *were* Publicis.

Respect sometimes works much, much better than money or tricks. When you are honest you have integrity and a genuine respect for people. They feel it, they understand it, and most of the time you have a natural bond that you can build upon. So Saatchi & Saatchi remains Saatchis, but they are also Publicis, and this has worked beautifully.

The integration of an agency or a company that you have bought is always a difficult process because there are many ways of merging; and if you don't do it right, you may well lose a very important part of what you have acquired. We should never forget that we are not acquiring buildings, factories, retail shops. We are acquiring office desks – and behind those desks are people. The people have to feel that the acquisition is the right thing for them. They have to feel that not only will they keep what they had, but there may also be the possibility of jumping to another level.

It is a new journey, but a journey they have already started, so it's not a disruption in their lives; it's not turning their lives upside down. It is the same situation, but with new objectives, new possibilities. Take Fallon, for example, which has a very strong corporate culture, a very strong image, with people who are considered the best. Obviously, when you are dealing with people who are considered the best, it will have some effect on their ego. We have to protect the ego to make sure that Fallon remains Fallon – to give it the possibility of achieving the dream. What we did was help Fallon to become a worldwide network, which previously it was not. So not only have we protected the integrity of the brand, but we have also given Fallon a new dream – and that is how the integration worked so well. 99

Executive Timeline Maurice Levy

1971	**Publicis**
	Joined what is now one of the world's largest advertising and media services conglomerates, initially to be responsible for data processing and information technology systems.
1973	*Corporate Secretary*
1976	*Managing Director*
1981	**Publicis Conseil**
	Chair and Chief Executive Officer
1986	**Publicis Groupe**
	Vice Chair
1988–present	*Chair* – Management Board

It is natural for people to be protective of their own areas of the business, but managers should avoid allowing separate 'silos' to develop. Horizontal communication allows staff to realize that they are part of a bigger picture and to share ideas and solutions.

11a

Breaking Down the Silos
Sir Richard Evans

Chairman, *United Utilities*; former Chairman, *British Aerospace*

My Career

 I have spent most of my working life in the aerospace business, but I came into it from a humble beginning. When I was starting out I never thought that I had received any guidance in the shaping and development of my career. Having become a bit smarter later on, I came to realize that there is a degree of organization within companies that tends to single people out and monitor their performance to see whether they have what it takes to move into more senior positions. Most of the moves I've made, particularly in the early stages of senior management, came as big surprises to me; they were not appointments that I'd ever imagined I would take at the time that I took them.

The really big move came when I was made Chief Executive of British Aerospace. I think it's fair to say that had I known at the time what I was walking into, I might have thought somewhat longer and harder about whether I should take the job. It was a seriously difficult assignment, with an immense number of problems that I didn't understand when I took on the role. Indeed, I don't think the company really understood quite what the issues were.

I spent longer in the Chief Executive's slot inside British Aerospace and then BAE Systems than I'd ever expected to. At that time the natural progression would have been for the Chief Executive to move on, and to take up a Chairmanship. I had never intended to become Chairman of British Aerospace; I took on the role on account of a set of domestic situations that arose for the then Chairman, Bob Bowman. Bob was an American, and he had to leave the UK to go back to the States. We didn't have time to undertake the usual search and selection process, so I came into the Chairmanship not as a part of conscious succession planning, but as an emergency interim appointment. A similar situation applied at United Utilities. I had been a Non-executive Director at United Utilities for a relatively short period of time when, tragically, the then Chairman of the company died very suddenly. My home was, and still is, in the northwest of England, where United Utilities is based. After first testing the market, the Board asked me if I would step up from my Non-executive position to become Chairman of the company.

I finished up at the top of two FTSE 100 companies via a set of circumstances that were complete chance. I had originally anticipated that, having finished my term as Chief Executive in British Aerospace, I would be able to regain control of my life and spend more time with my wife and family. That's still what I'm trying to achieve, but it's not proving to be as easy a I had expected.

Sir Richard Evans

Chairman, *United Utilities*; former Chairman, *British Aerospace*

Breaking Down the Silos

Organizations need structures to enable them to operate, and management needs structure in order to clarify where the boundaries of responsibility lie; but you can't afford to allow an organization to use structure as an excuse for poor management.

It's very easy for management to want to reside in its own comfort zones; that's why in a lot of organizations you tend to find 'silos' developing. However carefully you try to manage the structure of the business, people will gravitate naturally towards their own particular area; they will tend to build walls around it and then consider it their own piece of turf.

I try to deal with this by talking to the middle management guys in particular. They may not be as close to the corporate end of the business as I am, so it needs to be explained that, generally speaking, there's only one share price for the company; they may happen to work in subsidiary A or subsidiary B, but there is no separate share price for that business. There is only one share price for the company as a whole, and the fact that a manager happens to work in a particular subsection of the business doesn't in any way mitigate the responsibility that all managers have to look after the interests of the group.

People who get into the 'silo mentality' are forgetting that a major part of their management responsibility is to take an interest in the business as a whole, because ultimately that is how the company is valued.

Sir Richard Evans

If you can find a way of sharing information – by pushing down the walls of the silo and getting a horizontal form of communication working across the group – you'll suddenly discover that all sorts of things are possible.

I've seen many examples of this behaviour, particularly during my career in the aerospace business. I lived through a pretty turbulent time, having moved into a senior management position immediately after the company had been nationalized, and then taking it through into the privatization period. In that brief period – and it really was a very, very short period of time – I inherited a whole host of companies whose origins and heritages went back to the earliest days of powered flight. People were immensely proud of their heritage and the area of the business they were associated with – and quite rightly so. However, these individual businesses had been brought together as part of a single company, and when I started trying to weld them into a single entity there was immense resistance.

The people who had worked for these individual companies did not believe they were now working, in this particular case, for a company called British Aerospace. If I visited

Hatfield, I was considered to be working for De Havilland; if I travelled to Weybridge, I was working for the Vickers Airplane Company; if I went to Manchester, I was working for AV Rowe; at Bristol I was regarded as working for the Bristol Airplane Company. Nobody in these separate pieces of the organization had any interest in the business outside their own silo. I went through that period attempting to knock down the walls of the individual silos, trying to get people to see the bigger picture and to understand that it was really important to share their knowledge across the whole of the group, to make the sum of the parts come to something greater.

I am constantly amazed that people who have worked within the same company for twenty or thirty years may never have met each other. When they do eventually meet for the first time they realize: 'This guy is not the enemy; he's not the person I'm competing with. The guy I'm competing with is the one who is selling product against us, into the marketplace.'

Silo mentality is often the result of an introverted management succession process: people come in at the bottom of the silo, they work their way up, and they get to the top of the silo. They don't move horizontally across the business as a whole. Once barriers start to be removed, people from different parts of the business begin to meet one another, and the horizontal communication process begins. People suddenly realize that the problems in business are identical for any organization, and that someone they've never met before, but who works for the same company, may share exactly the same problem that they have.

Another point to bear in mind is that solutions to many problems will already reside inside the organization, and it is possible to avoid spending an immense amount of energy, time and cost in constantly reinventing solutions to problems that your colleagues have already found a solution to. If you can find a way of sharing information – by pushing down the walls of the silo and getting a horizontal form of communication working across the group – you'll suddenly discover that all sorts of things are possible. Improvements can be delivered at a much lower cost than would otherwise have been the case. Once people begin to see the benefits, they will want to knock the walls of the silo down themselves.

Those who are in the front line of communication with customers and clients make a disproportionate contribution to the company, and it is important that all staff are valued and recognized by management and colleagues for the part they play in the business. Personal recognition for a job well done will have a lasting impact.

Value Front-line Contributions

Mobilizing your people and getting them to march in the same direction that you're trying to head in are important issues.

I've always been pretty lucky in that I've worked in businesses that have employed large numbers of people, from 50,000 up to about 150,000. Mobilizing your people and getting them to march in the same direction that you're trying to head in are important issues.

People need to be recognized. In today's world people usually equate recognition with remuneration. Clearly everyone needs to have enough money to live on, and to have enough left over for extras – that's why they go to work – but in many ways recognition is not about money, it's about a lot of other things. Those who need particular recognition are the people who make a disproportionate contribution to the company.

I have a story that I used to tell the senior management team during one period of my career. In order to make a point at the management conferences, I would say: 'The most important people who work for me are the telephonists, the receptionists and the chauffeurs.' I would say this to an audience of highly educated engineers, who were PhD-qualified and capable of designing complete aircraft, supersonics, and every other aspect of flight you could think of. There would always be a sharp intake of breath when I said this, as they thought to themselves: 'How can the receptionist or the telephonist be more important than I am?'

I would explain that everybody who makes contact with our organization usually speaks first to a telephonist. If a client calls the switchboard, and the telephone rings twenty-five times before a surly person answers, asking 'What do you want?' the client will remember that. If the first time a visitor arrives at reception in one of our organizations the area is littered with used polystyrene cups and copies of last year's *National Geographic* magazines on the table, it will send a negative message. If, on the other hand, the area is clean and tidy, the receptionist is welcoming, and makes the visitor feel comfortable, they will have a positive first impression of the company.

The visitor can then meet the engineers and have a wonderfully stimulating discussion on something like the merits of fluid dynamics, or the plan of a wing-foil, but if, when they go back out to reception, the receptionist's attitude is dismissive or rude, the visitor won't remember the conversation they had with the engineer – stimulating though it may have been; the stronger impression will have been left by the receptionist, and it will stick.

Whichever part of the company I am visiting, I try to call in to the telephone exchange to speak to the people because they have a stressful job. Likewise I always like to look into the reception areas in order to remind the people working there how important they are. It's a form of recognition. It has nothing to do with money or anything else financial. Just being able to look a person in the eye and say: 'I think you're doing a great job. Well done,' is a form of recognition that those individuals will remember. It is amazing what the little phrase 'Well done' means to people.

In many ways, recognition is not about money, it's about a lot of other things.

Of course, the company has to deliver all the other things that go with verbal recognition, such as providing the right working conditions and the tools to do the job, so that the workplace is comfortable and somewhere people will want to be. It is also important to make the work interesting. However, the most important thing is to make sure that people understand that you value them. If you value them, they will value you, they will want to work with you and they will want to be part of the team.

When it comes to making an impression on clients and customers, receptionists, telephonists and others with service skills make a disproportionate contribution to the company. Yet many people inside the organization never actually recognize it.

Executive Timeline Sir Richard Evans

1960	**Ministry of Transport and Civil Aviation**
1967	**Ferranti**
	Government Contracts Officer
	Ferranti was a global organization known for technological innovation. It closed in 1994 after one hundred years of trading.
1969	**British Aircraft Corporation**
	Joined the Military Aircraft Division.
1978	*Commercial Director* – Warton Division, British Aerospace (BAe)
1981	*Assistant Managing Director* – Warton Division
1983–1986	*Deputy Managing Director*
	Appointed following BAe Aircraft Group managerial changes.
1986	*Deputy Managing Director (and Managing Director Designate)* – British Aerospace Military Aircraft Division
1987	*Marketing Director* – British Aerospace
	Appointed to the Board.
1988	*Chairman* – British Aerospace Defence companies
1990	*Chief Executive* – British Aerospace
1996	Knighted in the 1996 Queen's Birthday Honours.
1997	**United Utilities**
	Joined the Board as a Non-executive Director. United Utilities manages water and wastewater networks in Wales and wastewater treatment facilities in Scotland.
1998–2004	*Chairman* – British Aerospace
	Continued to chair the company when it became BAE Systems following the merger with Marconi Electronic Systems. Retired from this position in July 2004, but continues to support the company in an advisory capacity.
2001–present	**United Utilities**
	Chairman

Leadership is about getting things done and empowering people to do things, rather than issuing autocratic directives. So involve the people who are key to setting the direction of a company, as this will be instrumental in its success.

12   **Involve Key People in Setting Direction**
Don Cruickshank

Former Chairman, *London Stock Exchange*

My Career

 I moved into industry in 1967 and worked for Alcan Aluminium. It was a Canadian company with a management style quite different from the style in British industry at that time. After that I became one of the first two non-US MBAs recruited by McKinsey into their London office and spent about five years there. Then came a completely random jump into newspapers. I stayed in the newspaper industry until 1980, when, following my unsuccessful attempt with Harold Evans to lead a management buyout of *The Sunday Times*, Rupert Murdoch bought *The Times* and *The Sunday Times*. That was a good experience. Two further jobs in media followed: the first with Pearson, and then, in 1984, I joined Richard Branson as Managing Director of the Virgin Group, later becoming Managing Director of the Entertainment and Music Group, which became a public company. I also helped Richard with his private businesses, including the airline.

During the same period, at the age of forty-three, I became Chairman of Wandsworth Health Authority in London. That got me involved in the politics of health and healthcare. When Richard brought his companies back into private ownership in 1989, that experience encouraged me to see whether my management skills or lessons learned could be deployed to effect in the National Health Service. I went to Scotland to become Chief Executive of the NHS in Scotland.

While based in Scotland I was headhunted in 1993 by Michael Heseltine to become Director General of Telecoms at Oftel.

I worked there for five years. After that I held two odd jobs: conducting a review of competition in retail banking in the UK for Gordon Brown, the Chancellor of the Exchequer – that was good fun, not least because I spent eighteen months inside HM Treasury – and leading the UK's Y2K campaign.

Following that, as has happened a number of times in my career for reasons I don't properly understand, I was headhunted to be Chairman of the London Stock Exchange. I had no relevant financial services experience, but presumably offered some talent and potential. I achieved what I was asked to achieve and left the role in July 2003. Since then I've been Chairman of Scottish Media Group, Chairman of the publishing company Taylor & Francis, and for the first time have become Chairman of a software company in the private capital world. I took this last role because I wanted to get direct experience of where science and technology are taking us and I'm working with a team of thirty-year-olds, which is very good for me.

Don Cruickshank

Former Chairman, *London Stock Exchange*

Involve Key People in Setting Direction

One of the key lessons that I have learnt in business is the importance of involving the appropriate staff in setting the direction of the company. During the time I was Chief Executive of the National Health Service in Scotland there was a great deal of debate over the issue of *in-vitro* fertilization (IVF). Questions were being asked: What was the role of the National Health Service in deciding who should have IVF? Should it be priced? Should it be free? What precisely should be free? What were the rights of families? All the assembled wisdom of the management team in the Scottish Office was getting us absolutely nowhere because we were shying away from some of the main issues.

In effect, we gave the problem to the Royal College of Obstetricians and Gynaecologists. We said to them: 'Here's the issue. What we want from you is a set of protocols, i.e. what rights does a woman have to various classes of treatment? How often and in what circumstances should *in-vitro* fertilization be offered?' and so on.

This approach was seen to be highly risky by my management team in the Scottish Office and by ministers, but it turned

One of the key lessons that I have learnt in business is the importance of involving the appropriate staff in setting the direction of the company.

Good leadership is about getting things done, and getting people's involvement in making that happen, rather than simply directing them in an autocratic fashion.

out to be absolutely right. What emerged from the Royal College was a set of rules that had the authority of the medical profession. That meant that all the doctors who were operating the service were prepared to conform to the guidelines, even to the extent of some of them stopping practising certain procedures and referring individuals to centres of excellence. Such an outcome was achieved by involving appropriate staff in an issue that initially was not even seen to be a responsibility of the Health Service.

The experience reinforced for me the importance of involving staff in setting the direction of an organization. It also made me realize how resistant I was, and certainly my colleagues were, to letting that happen. It reminded me of the ways in which we had tried to avoid it by pretending that we could solve things ourselves. Leaders often can't solve things by themselves; good leadership is about getting things done, and getting people's involvement in making that happen, rather than simply directing them in an autocratic fashion.

Executive Timeline Don Cruickshank

1967–1970	**Alcan Aluminium** *Finance, systems and marketing projects work.* A Canadian aluminium company.
1972–1977	**McKinsey & Co Inc** *Consultant* A management consultancy.
1977–1980	**Times Newspapers** *Commercial Director*
1979–1980	***The Sunday Times*** *General Manager*
1980–1983	**Pearson plc** *Managing Director – Finance, Administration, Planning* Pearson is a media group, which at this time included: the *Financial Times*, Goldcrest, Longman and Penguin.
1984–1989	**Virgin Group plc** *Managing Director* *Managing Director – Entertainment and Music Group*
1986–1989	**Wandsworth Health Authority** *Chairman*
1989–1993	**National Health Service, Scotland** *Chief Executive*
1993–1998	**Oftel** *Director-General – Telecommunications* Oftel was the the UK's industry regulator.
1997–2000	Led the Y2K campaign, the UK government's millennium bug campaign.
1998–2000	**HM Treasury** *Chairman* Supervised 'Competition in UK Banking: A Report to The Chancellor of the Exchequer', published 2000.
2000–2003	**London Stock Exchange** *Chairman*
2003–2004	**The Scottish Media Group plc** *Chairman*

> Succession planning should always be high on a Chief Executive's agenda. Careful selection of candidates, coupled with proper handover preparation, is a key ingredient for a seamless transition.

13   **Succession Planning**
Lord MacLaurin

Chairman, *Vodafone Group*; former Chairman, *Tesco*

My Career

 My schooldays were among the most important times of my life. I went to school in Malvern in Worcestershire and was a boarder between the ages of thirteen and eighteen. I was a proficient sportsman, so was fortunate enough to captain the cricket side, the soccer side and the rugger side for my last two years there. By that means I started to learn about people and their strengths and weaknesses. Malvern gave me a very, very good education, which sent me off into the wide world. From there I could have gone to university, but instead I had to do National Service. I joined the Air Force, where I again played soccer and cricket and didn't really serve our country very well. I was one of the last lot to go into National Service and I found it was good fun. I started to meet all sorts of different people and suddenly felt I was getting into the real world. The experience taught me a lot about human nature and mixing with and understanding people.

I joined Tesco in 1959 as their first trainee, and worked my way through the operation to become Managing Director and then Chairman. I left Tesco in 1997 to join Vodafone, and became Chairman in 1999. I'm now also Chair of the Governors of my old school. In this day and age it is very unusual for somebody to spend the majority of their working life, nearly forty years in my case, in one company, starting first as a trainee and finishing up as Chairman. These days, people chop and change their jobs quite regularly, but I had the great privilege of working with a company and turning it round, and creating probably one of the strongest retail brands in this country today. Tesco is a major force in world retailing. Then to have the opportunity to work with Chris Gent to create a world business at Vodafone has meant that I have had a very interesting career. I'm very lucky in lots of ways, and the experience has been thoroughly enjoyable.

Lord MacLaurin

Chairman, *Vodafone Group*; former Chairman, *Tesco*

Succession planning is very, very important. The Managing Director, the Deputy Chairman and I each started to think seriously about succession planning two years before any of us left Tesco, and we executed our plans very well.

Planning your succession is part of a mindset. You need to set yourself a date and say: 'I believe I can make a positive contribution to this company until XXXX.' Then you need to think about how you're going to achieve your aims, whether you're going to have to source external help to plan your succession, or whether you have sufficient skill within the company. My preference has always been to develop my own people.

Succession planning is very, very important. The Managing Director, the Deputy Chairman and I each started to think seriously about succession planning two years before any of us left Tesco and we executed our plans very well. When I left, Terry Leahy took over as the Chief Executive, and it was an absolutely seamless transition. Terry had been with us for about fifteen years before we noted him, together with a number of others in the group, as a possible high-flyer. We placed these potentially key players strategically around the business so they each knew exactly what was happening.

Bringing somebody from inside to the top job was a great move.

About eighteen months before I was leaving, I went to the City to say: 'I'm going. I'm going on this date and Terry Leahy is taking over.' During my final nine months or so, Terry ran the business and I acted as his mentor. We were very close. I then moved out and he took over. I think it serves as a very good case study for anybody wanting a seamless changeover.

When I left Tesco I joined Vodafone as a Non-executive Director, and then became Chairman in 2000 when the incumbent stepped down. I worked very closely with Chris Gent to develop Vodafone Newbury from a small regional company to an international force. In 1999 we were probably sixtieth or seventieth in the FTSE index – really quite small. In two or three years we achieved two remarkable takeovers: first AirTouch in San Francisco, which gave us a big holding in North America and also enhanced our position in Europe because AirTouch had big shareholdings in a number of European companies; then we took over the German company Mannesmann. In just two or three years, Vodafone grew from being a small mobile business in Newbury to one of the biggest companies in the world.

Chris Gent did for Vodafone what I had done for Tesco. About a year before he left the company he came to me to discuss

The bad managers are the ones who stay on too long, or those who don't really make a major contribution to the business.

how we were going to find his successor. We had a conference with the main Board, and I invited any of the Executive or Non-executive Directors to apply to me if they wanted to be considered. We then hired a headhunter to look outside the company. My small nominations committee interviewed four people, and Arun Sarin, the internal candidate, was the clear leader on every count. He had been an executive with AirTouch; he had then worked for Vodafone AirTouch for a while; he was a Non-executive Director, and he's come back with great success as Chief Executive. Bringing somebody from inside to the top job was a great move. Although we also looked outside, we found nobody of sufficient calibre to challenge the decision to appoint Arun.

My job in Vodafone at the moment is to run the Board, to engage Non-executive Directors, to spend a lot of time in the business with the Executive Directors, and, while I'm doing that, ascertain the value of the Executive Directors, with a mind to having a shortlist of people ready for when Arun decides to leave. If you're a good manager, you should be thinking about the line of succession all the time. The bad managers are the ones who stay on too long, or those

If you're good, you've got to make a major contribution to the business and then move on. You have to keep moving on.

who don't really make a major contribution to the business. If you're good, you've got to make a major contribution to the business and then move on. You have to keep moving on. 99

1959	**Tesco**
	Management Trainee
	Joined the supermarket chain as its first management trainee.
1970	Appointed to the Board of Directors.
1973–1985	*Managing Director*
1985–1997	*Chairman*
1989	Awarded a knighthood.
1996	Awarded a life peerage.
1997	**Vodafone Group**
	Appointed to the Board of Directors.
2000–present	*Chairman*
	Chairman of the Nominations and Governance Committee
	Member of the Remuneration Committee

There is no substitute for experience – learn more from the best minds in business

Did you know that Fifty Lessons has created a must-have digital library containing more than 350 *filmed* business lessons that can be viewed online, from home or in your office?

Through Fifty Lessons you can:

- Experience first-hand the real-life learning of some of the most influential business leaders of our time.
- Gain access to a vast array of concise lessons covering ove thirty-five key leadership and management topics.
- Benefit from decades of hard-won learning and experience.

To subscribe to Fifty Lessons, and to take advantage of our special reader discount, please visit www.fiftylessons.com/readeroffer for details.

We also offer customized solutions for larger organizations, from providing lessons on DVD and print to distributing tailored lesson packages via email and corporate intranets. For further information please visit www.fiftylessons.com or

For corporate sales enquiries please contact:

BBC Worldwide Learning
Woodlands
80 Wood Lane
London
W12 0TT
United Kingdom
Tel: +44 (0)20 8433 1641
Fax: +44 (0)20 8433 2916
Email:
corporate.sales @bbc.co.uk

For any other enquiries please contact:

Fifty Lessons
Fitzroy House
11 Chenies Street
London
WC1E 7EY
United Kingdom
Tel: +44 (0)20 7636 477
Fax: +44 (0)20 7636 488
Email:
info@fiftylessons.com